# Comfort Cruise, a Voyage to Adventure

## Travel Journal

### Activinotes

**Activinotes**

DAILY JOURNALS, PLANNERS, NOTEBOOKS AND OTHER BLANK BOOKS

Copyright 2016

# Travel Journal

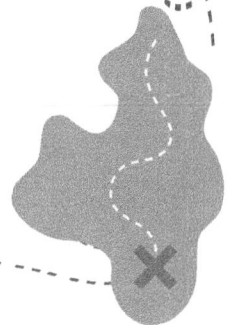

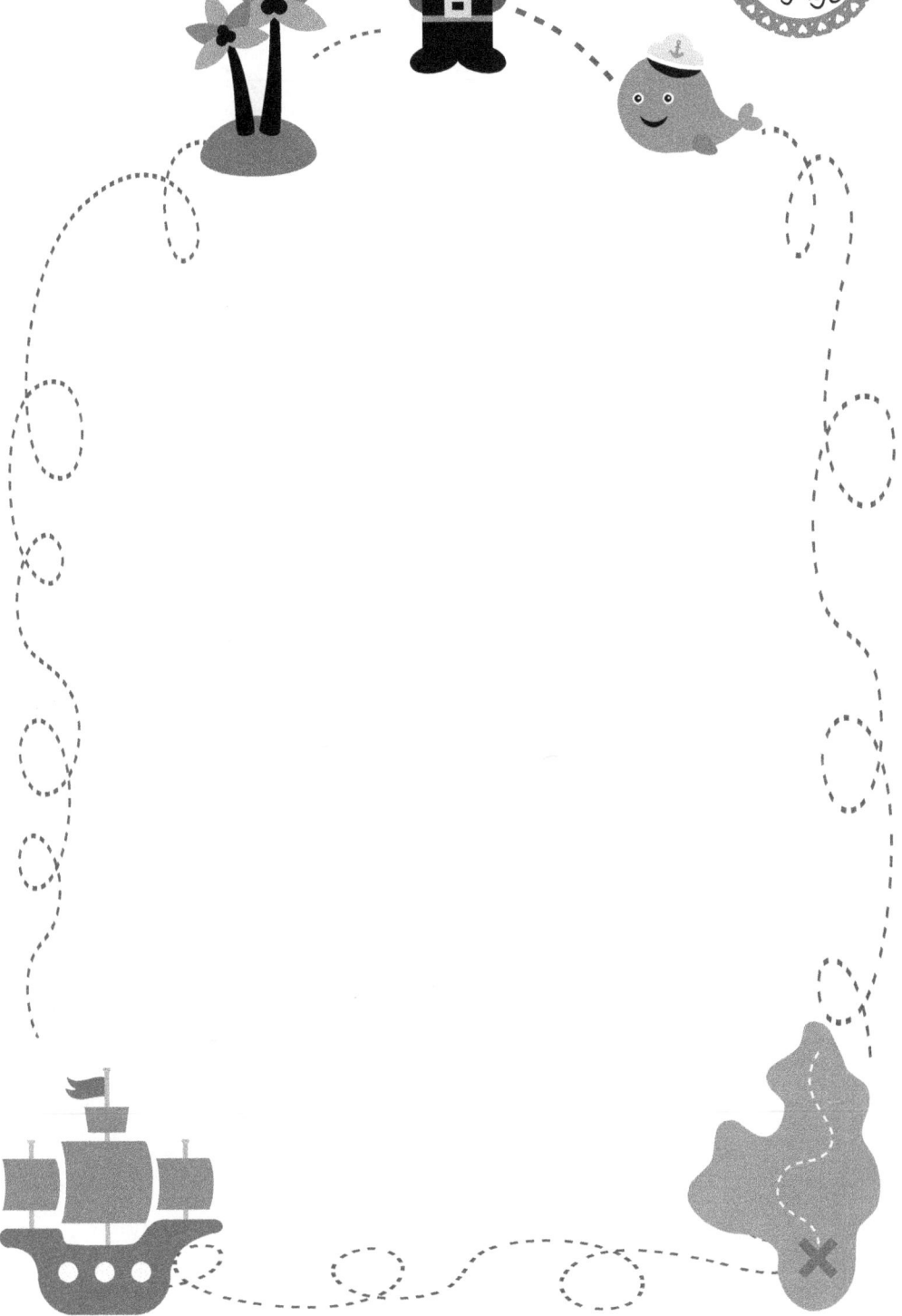

bon ♡ Voyage

# Travel Journal

bon Voyage

## Things to See & Do:

- ☐ ........................................................
- ☐ ........................................................
- ☐ ........................................................
- ☐ ........................................................
- ☐ ........................................................
- ☐ ........................................................
- ☐ ........................................................
- ☐ ........................................................
- ☐ ........................................................
- ☐ ........................................................

## Things to Observe :

- ☐ ........................................................
- ☐ ........................................................
- ☐ ........................................................
- ☐ ........................................................
- ☐ ........................................................
- ☐ ........................................................
- ☐ ........................................................

## Adventures to Have :

- ☐ ........................................................
- ☐ ........................................................
- ☐ ........................................................
- ☐ ........................................................
- ☐ ........................................................
- ☐ ........................................................
- ☐ ........................................................

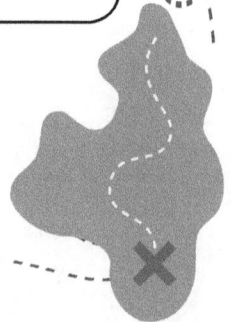

# Travel Journal

## Places to Mingle :

☐ ................................................
☐ ................................................
☐ ................................................
☐ ................................................
☐ ................................................
☐ ................................................

## Shops to Visit :

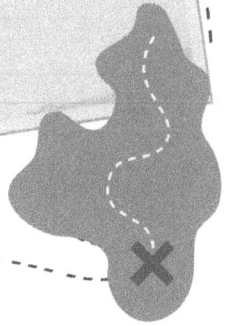

☐ ................................................
☐ ................................................
☐ ................................................
☐ ................................................
☐ ................................................
☐ ................................................
☐ ................................................

place your
photo here

place your
photo here

# Travel Journal

bon Voyage

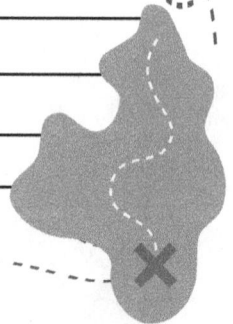

# Travel Journal

bon ♡ Voyage

## Things to See & Do:

- ☐ .............................................................
- ☐ .............................................................
- ☐ .............................................................
- ☐ .............................................................
- ☐ .............................................................
- ☐ .............................................................
- ☐ .............................................................
- ☐ .............................................................
- ☐ .............................................................
- ☐ .............................................................

## Adventures to Have :

- ☐ ...........................................
- ☐ ...........................................
- ☐ ...........................................
- ☐ ...........................................
- ☐ ...........................................
- ☐ ...........................................
- ☐ ...........................................

## Things to Observe :

- ☐ ...........................................
- ☐ ...........................................
- ☐ ...........................................
- ☐ ...........................................
- ☐ ...........................................
- ☐ ...........................................

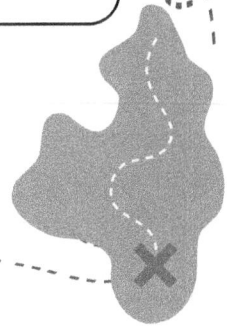

# Travel Journal

bon ♡ Voyage

## Places to Mingle :

- ☐ ......................................
- ☐ ......................................
- ☐ ......................................
- ☐ ......................................
- ☐ ......................................
- ☐ ......................................
- ☐ ......................................

## Shops to Visit :

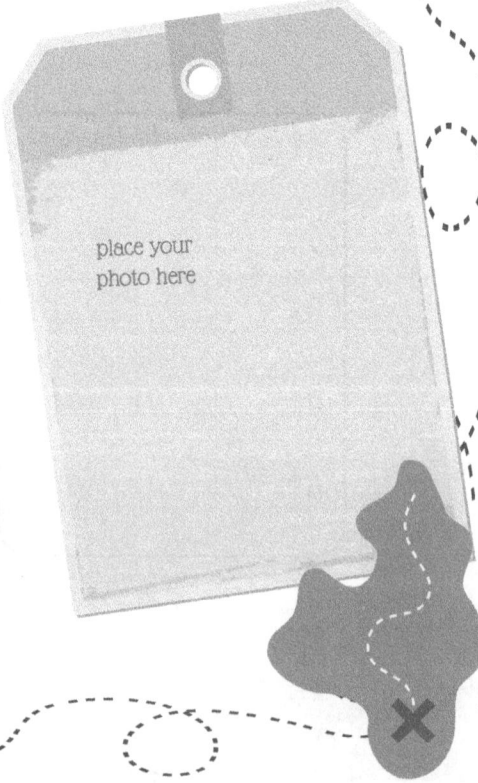

- ☐ ......................................
- ☐ ......................................
- ☐ ......................................
- ☐ ......................................
- ☐ ......................................
- ☐ ......................................
- ☐ ......................................

place your
photo here

place your
photo here

# Travel Journal

_____

_____

_____

_____

_____

_____

_____

_____

_____

_____

_____

_____

_____

_____

_____

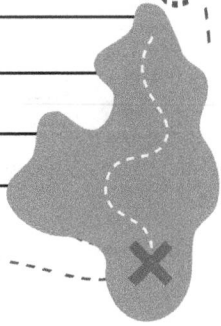

# Travel Journal

## Things to See & Do:

- [ ] ........................................................
- [ ] ........................................................
- [ ] ........................................................
- [ ] ........................................................
- [ ] ........................................................
- [ ] ........................................................
- [ ] ........................................................
- [ ] ........................................................
- [ ] ........................................................
- [ ] ........................................................

## Adventures to Have :

- [ ] ........................................
- [ ] ........................................
- [ ] ........................................
- [ ] ........................................
- [ ] ........................................
- [ ] ........................................
- [ ] ........................................

## Things to Observe :

- [ ] ........................................
- [ ] ........................................
- [ ] ........................................
- [ ] ........................................
- [ ] ........................................
- [ ] ........................................
- [ ] ........................................

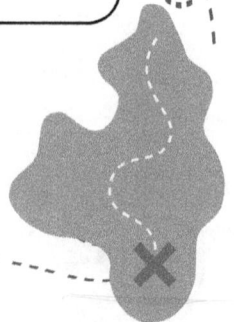

bon Voyage

# Travel Journal

## Places to Mingle :

☐ .....................................
☐ .....................................
☐ .....................................
☐ .....................................
☐ .....................................
☐ .....................................
☐ .....................................

## Shops to Visit :

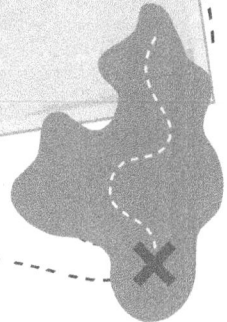

☐ .....................................
☐ .....................................
☐ .....................................
☐ .....................................
☐ .....................................
☐ .....................................
☐ .....................................

place your
photo here

place your
photo here

# Travel Journal

bon
Voyage

_____
_____
_____
_____
_____
_____
_____
_____
_____
_____
_____
_____
_____
_____
_____

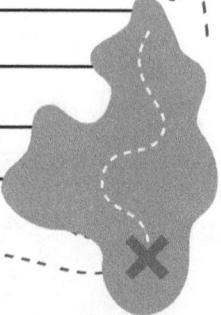

# Travel Journal

## Things to See & Do:

- ☐ .................................................
- ☐ .................................................
- ☐ .................................................
- ☐ .................................................
- ☐ .................................................
- ☐ .................................................
- ☐ .................................................
- ☐ .................................................
- ☐ .................................................
- ☐ .................................................

### Things to Observe :

- ☐ ...........................................
- ☐ ...........................................
- ☐ ...........................................
- ☐ ...........................................
- ☐ ...........................................
- ☐ ...........................................

### Adventures to Have :

- ☐ ...........................................
- ☐ ...........................................
- ☐ ...........................................
- ☐ ...........................................
- ☐ ...........................................
- ☐ ...........................................
- ☐

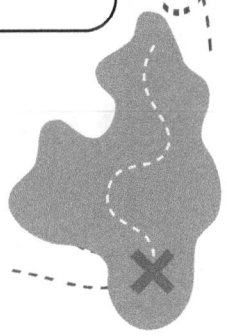

# Travel Journal

bon ♡ Voyage

## Places to Mingle :

☐ ................................
☐ ................................
☐ ................................
☐ ................................
☐ ................................
☐ ................................
☐ ................................

## Shops to Visit :

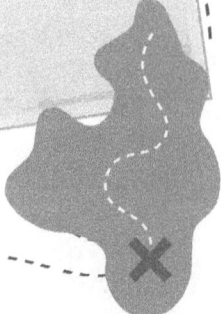

☐ ................................
☐ ................................
☐ ................................
☐ ................................
☐ ................................
☐ ................................
☐ ................................

place your
photo here

place your
photo here

# Travel Journal

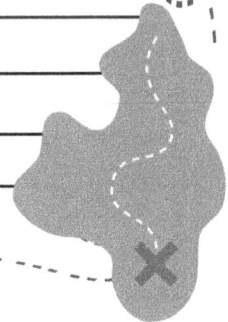

# Travel Journal

bon♡ Voyage

## Things to See & Do.

- ☐ ........................................................
- ☐ ........................................................
- ☐ ........................................................
- ☐ ........................................................
- ☐ ........................................................
- ☐ ........................................................
- ☐ ........................................................
- ☐ ........................................................
- ☐ ........................................................
- ☐ ........................................................

## Adventures to Have :

- ☐ ........................................
- ☐ ........................................
- ☐ ........................................
- ☐ ........................................
- ☐ ........................................
- ☐ ........................................
- ☐ ........................................

## Things to Observe :

- ☐ ........................................
- ☐ ........................................
- ☐ ........................................
- ☐ ........................................
- ☐ ........................................
- ☐ ........................................
- ☐ ........................................

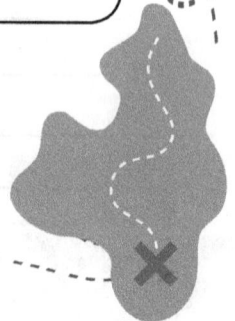

# Travel Journal

bon ♡ Voyage

## Places to Mingle :

☐ .........................................
☐ .........................................
☐ .........................................
☐ .........................................
☐ .........................................
☐ .........................................

## Shops to Visit :

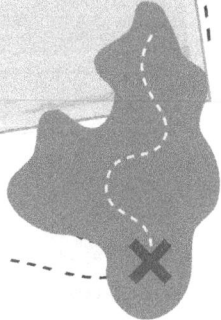

☐ .........................................
☐ .........................................
☐ .........................................
☐ .........................................
☐ .........................................
☐ .........................................
☐ .........................................

place your
photo here

place your
photo here

# Travel Journal

bon Voyage

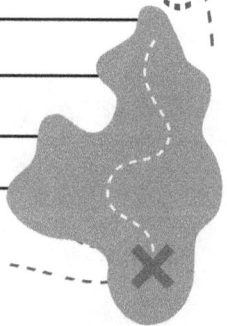

# Travel Journal

## Things to See & Do:

- ☐ ..............................................................
- ☐ ..............................................................
- ☐ ..............................................................
- ☐ ..............................................................
- ☐ ..............................................................
- ☐ ..............................................................
- ☐ ..............................................................
- ☐ ..............................................................
- ☐ ..............................................................
- ☐ ..............................................................

## Adventures to Have :

- ☐ ....................................
- ☐ ....................................
- ☐ ....................................
- ☐ ....................................
- ☐ ....................................
- ☐ ....................................
- ☐ ....................................

## Things to Observe :

- ☐ ....................................
- ☐ ....................................
- ☐ ....................................
- ☐ ....................................
- ☐ ....................................
- ☐ ....................................

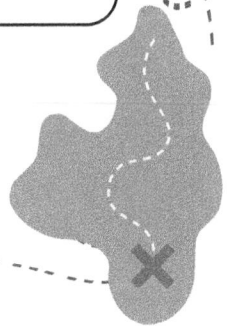

# Travel Journal

bon ♡ Voyage

## Places to Mingle :

- ☐ .............................................
- ☐ .............................................
- ☐ .............................................
- ☐ .............................................
- ☐ .............................................
- ☐ .............................................
- ☐ .............................................

## Shops to Visit :

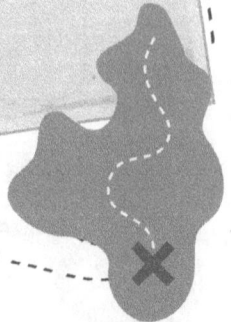

- ☐ .............................................
- ☐ .............................................
- ☐ .............................................
- ☐ .............................................
- ☐ .............................................
- ☐ .............................................
- ☐ .............................................

place your
photo here

place your
photo here

# Travel Journal

bon Voyage

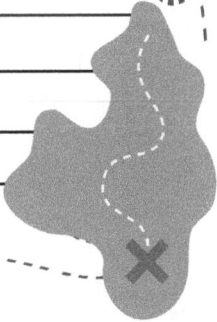

# Travel Journal

bon ♡ Voyage

## Things to See & Do:

- ☐ .......................................................................
- ☐ .......................................................................
- ☐ .......................................................................
- ☐ .......................................................................
- ☐ .......................................................................
- ☐ .......................................................................
- ☐ .......................................................................
- ☐ .......................................................................
- ☐ .......................................................................
- ☐ .......................................................................

## Adventures to Have :

- ☐ ........................................
- ☐ ........................................
- ☐ ........................................
- ☐ ........................................
- ☐ ........................................
- ☐ ........................................
- ☐ ........................................

## Things to Observe :

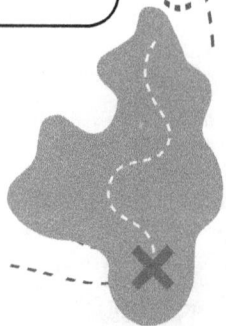

- ☐ ........................................
- ☐ ........................................
- ☐ ........................................
- ☐ ........................................
- ☐ ........................................
- ☐ ........................................

# Travel Journal

bon♡ Voyage

## Shops to Visit :

- ☐ ...........................................................
- ☐ ...........................................................
- ☐ ...........................................................
- ☐ ...........................................................
- ☐ ...........................................................
- ☐ ...........................................................
- ☐ ...........................................................

## Places to Mingle :

- ☐ ...........................................................
- ☐ ...........................................................
- ☐ ...........................................................
- ☐ ...........................................................
- ☐ ...........................................................
- ☐ ...........................................................

place your
photo here

place your
photo here

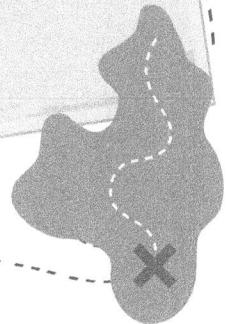

# Travel Journal

_____

_____

_____

_____

_____

_____

_____

_____

_____

_____

_____

_____

_____

_____

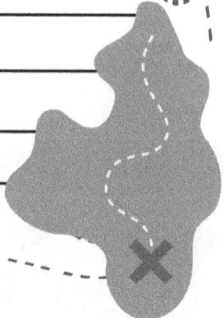

# Travel Journal

## Things to See & Do:

- ☐ .................................................
- ☐ .................................................
- ☐ .................................................
- ☐ .................................................
- ☐ .................................................
- ☐ .................................................
- ☐ .................................................
- ☐ .................................................
- ☐ .................................................
- ☐ .................................................

## Adventures to Have :

- ☐ ................................
- ☐ ................................
- ☐ ................................
- ☐ ................................
- ☐ ................................
- ☐ ................................
- ☐ ................................

## Things to Observe :

- ☐ ................................
- ☐ ................................
- ☐ ................................
- ☐ ................................
- ☐ ................................
- ☐ ................................
- ☐ ................................

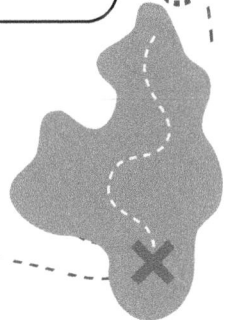

# Travel Journal

## Places to Mingle :

- ☐ ......................................
- ☐ ......................................
- ☐ ......................................
- ☐ ......................................
- ☐ ......................................
- ☐ ......................................

## Shops to Visit :

- ☐ ......................................
- ☐ ......................................
- ☐ ......................................
- ☐ ......................................
- ☐ ......................................
- ☐ ......................................
- ☐ ......................................

bon Voyage

place your
photo here

place your
photo here

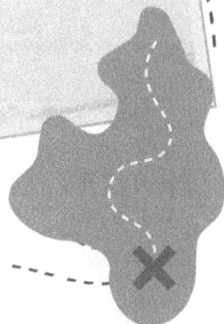

# Travel Journal

_____
_____
_____
_____
_____
_____
_____
_____
_____
_____
_____
_____
_____
_____
_____
_____

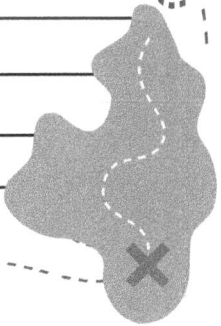

# Travel Journal

## Things to See & Do.

- ☐ .................................................................
- ☐ .................................................................
- ☐ .................................................................
- ☐ .................................................................
- ☐ .................................................................
- ☐ .................................................................
- ☐ .................................................................
- ☐ .................................................................
- ☐ .................................................................
- ☐ .................................................................

## Adventures to Have :

- ☐ .................................................
- ☐ .................................................
- ☐ .................................................
- ☐ .................................................
- ☐ .................................................
- ☐ .................................................
- ☐ .................................................

## Things to Observe :

- ☐ .................................................
- ☐ .................................................
- ☐ .................................................
- ☐ .................................................
- ☐ .................................................
- ☐ .................................................
- ☐ .................................................

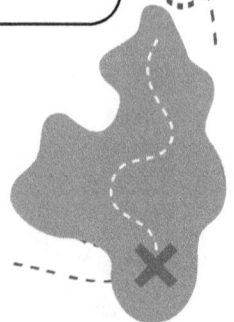

bon Voyage

# Travel Journal

bon ♡ Voyage

## Places to Mingle :

- ☐ .................................
- ☐ .................................
- ☐ .................................
- ☐ .................................
- ☐ .................................
- ☐ .................................
- ☐ .................................

## Shops to Visit :

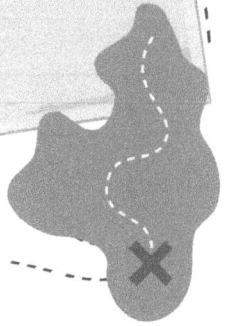

- ☐ .................................
- ☐ .................................
- ☐ .................................
- ☐ .................................
- ☐ .................................
- ☐ .................................
- ☐ .................................

place your
photo here

place your
photo here

# Travel Journal

bon♡ Voyage

# Travel Journal

bon Voyage

## Things to See & Do:

- ☐ ....................................................
- ☐ ....................................................
- ☐ ....................................................
- ☐ ....................................................
- ☐ ....................................................
- ☐ ....................................................
- ☐ ....................................................
- ☐ ....................................................
- ☐ ....................................................
- ☐ ....................................................

## Adventures to Have :

- ☐ ....................................
- ☐ ....................................
- ☐ ....................................
- ☐ ....................................
- ☐ ....................................
- ☐ ....................................
- ☐ ....................................

## Things to Observe :

- ☐ ....................................
- ☐ ....................................
- ☐ ....................................
- ☐ ....................................
- ☐ ....................................
- ☐ ....................................

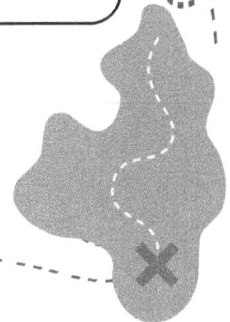

# Travel Journal

bon Voyage

## Places to Mingle :

- ☐ .............................
- ☐ .............................
- ☐ .............................
- ☐ .............................
- ☐ .............................
- ☐ .............................
- ☐ .............................

## Shops to Visit :

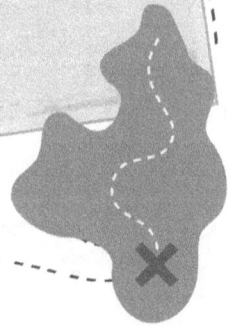

- ☐ .............................
- ☐ .............................
- ☐ .............................
- ☐ .............................
- ☐ .............................
- ☐ .............................
- ☐ .............................

place your
photo here

place your
photo here

# Travel Journal

_____
_____
_____
_____
_____
_____
_____
_____
_____
_____
_____
_____
_____
_____
_____
_____

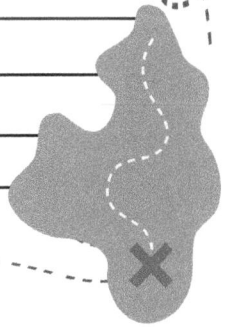

# Travel Journal

bon Voyage

## Things to See & Do:

- [ ] ................................................
- [ ] ................................................
- [ ] ................................................
- [ ] ................................................
- [ ] ................................................
- [ ] ................................................
- [ ] ................................................
- [ ] ................................................
- [ ] ................................................
- [ ] ................................................

## Adventures to Have:

- [ ] ................................
- [ ] ................................
- [ ] ................................
- [ ] ................................
- [ ] ................................
- [ ] ................................
- [ ] ................................

## Things to Observe:

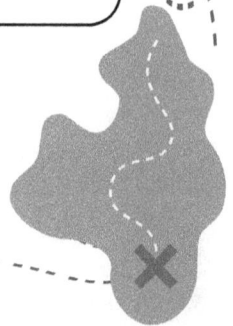

- [ ] ................................
- [ ] ................................
- [ ] ................................
- [ ] ................................
- [ ] ................................
- [ ] ................................

# Travel Journal

bon♡ Voyage

## Places to Mingle :

- ☐ ..........................................
- ☐ ..........................................
- ☐ ..........................................
- ☐ ..........................................
- ☐ ..........................................
- ☐ ..........................................
- ☐ ..........................................

## Shops to Visit :

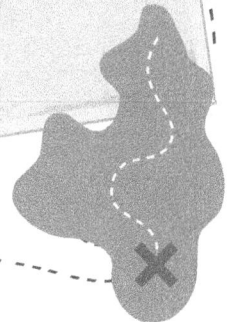

- ☐ ..........................................
- ☐ ..........................................
- ☐ ..........................................
- ☐ ..........................................
- ☐ ..........................................
- ☐ ..........................................
- ☐ ..........................................

place your
photo here

place your
photo here

# Travel Journal

bon Voyage

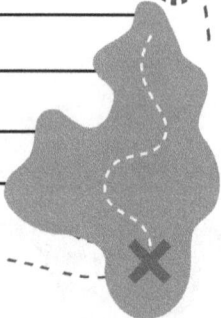

# Travel Journal

bon ♡ Voyage

### Things to See & Do:

- ☐ ...........................................................................
- ☐ ...........................................................................
- ☐ ...........................................................................
- ☐ ...........................................................................
- ☐ ...........................................................................
- ☐ ...........................................................................
- ☐ ...........................................................................
- ☐ ...........................................................................
- ☐ ...........................................................................
- ☐ ...........................................................................

### Things to Observe :

- ☐ ...........................................................
- ☐ ...........................................................
- ☐ ...........................................................
- ☐ ...........................................................
- ☐ ...........................................................
- ☐ ...........................................................
- ☐ ...........................................................

### Adventures to Have :

- ☐ ...........................................................
- ☐ ...........................................................
- ☐ ...........................................................
- ☐ ...........................................................
- ☐ ...........................................................
- ☐ ...........................................................

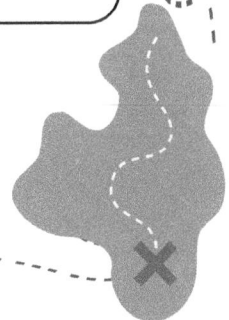

# Travel Journal

bon ♡ Voyage

## Places to Mingle :

- ☐ ..........................................
- ☐ ..........................................
- ☐ ..........................................
- ☐ ..........................................
- ☐ ..........................................
- ☐ ..........................................

## Shops to Visit :

- ☐ ..........................................
- ☐ ..........................................
- ☐ ..........................................
- ☐ ..........................................
- ☐ ..........................................
- ☐ ..........................................
- ☐ ..........................................

place your
photo here

place your
photo here

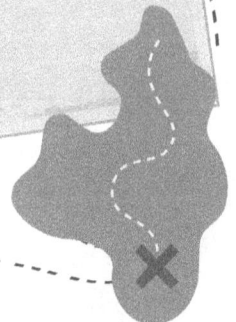

# Travel Journal

bon ♡
Voyage

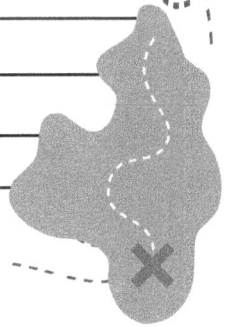

# Travel Journal

## Things to See & Do:

- ☐ ........................................................
- ☐ ........................................................
- ☐ ........................................................
- ☐ ........................................................
- ☐ ........................................................
- ☐ ........................................................
- ☐ ........................................................
- ☐ ........................................................
- ☐ ........................................................
- ☐ ........................................................

## Things to Observe :

- ☐ ........................................................
- ☐ ........................................................
- ☐ ........................................................
- ☐ ........................................................
- ☐ ........................................................
- ☐ ........................................................
- ☐ ........................................................

## Adventures to Have :

- ☐ ........................................................
- ☐ ........................................................
- ☐ ........................................................
- ☐ ........................................................
- ☐ ........................................................
- ☐ ........................................................
- ☐ ........................................................

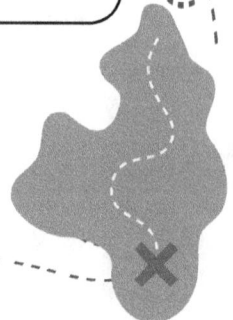

# Travel Journal

## Shops to Visit :

- ☐ .....................................................
- ☐ .....................................................
- ☐ .....................................................
- ☐ .....................................................
- ☐ .....................................................
- ☐ .....................................................
- ☐ .....................................................

## Places to Mingle :

- ☐ .....................................................
- ☐ .....................................................
- ☐ .....................................................
- ☐ .....................................................
- ☐ .....................................................
- ☐ .....................................................
- ☐ .....................................................

place your
photo here

place your
photo here

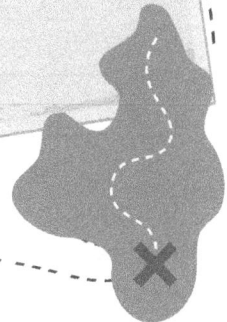

# Travel Journal

bon ♡ Voyage

# Travel Journal

bon ♡ Voyage

## Things to See & Do:

- ☐ .............................................................
- ☐ .............................................................
- ☐ .............................................................
- ☐ .............................................................
- ☐ .............................................................
- ☐ .............................................................
- ☐ .............................................................
- ☐ .............................................................
- ☐ .............................................................
- ☐ .............................................................

## Adventures to Have :

- ☐ ...........................................
- ☐ ...........................................
- ☐ ...........................................
- ☐ ...........................................
- ☐ ...........................................
- ☐ ...........................................
- ☐ ...........................................

## Things to Observe :

- ☐ ...........................................
- ☐ ...........................................
- ☐ ...........................................
- ☐ ...........................................
- ☐ ...........................................
- ☐ ...........................................
- ☐ ...........................................

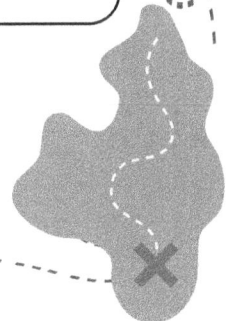

# Travel Journal

bon ♡ Voyage

## Places to Mingle :

- ☐ ....................................
- ☐ ....................................
- ☐ ....................................
- ☐ ....................................
- ☐ ....................................
- ☐ ....................................

## Shops to Visit :

- ☐ ....................................
- ☐ ....................................
- ☐ ....................................
- ☐ ....................................
- ☐ ....................................
- ☐ ....................................
- ☐ ....................................

place your
photo here

place your
photo here

# Travel Journal

_____

_____

_____

_____

_____

_____

_____

_____

_____

_____

_____

_____

_____

_____

_____

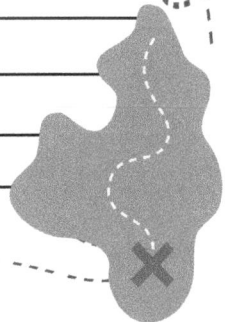

# Travel Journal

bon♡ Voyage

## Things to See & Do:

- ☐ .........................................................................
- ☐ .........................................................................
- ☐ .........................................................................
- ☐ .........................................................................
- ☐ .........................................................................
- ☐ .........................................................................
- ☐ .........................................................................
- ☐ .........................................................................
- ☐ .........................................................................
- ☐ .........................................................................

## Adventures to Have :

- ☐ ...........................................
- ☐ ...........................................
- ☐ ...........................................
- ☐ ...........................................
- ☐ ...........................................
- ☐ ...........................................
- ☐ ...........................................

## Things to Observe :

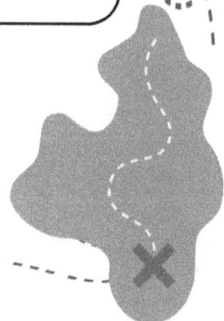

- ☐ ...........................................
- ☐ ...........................................
- ☐ ...........................................
- ☐ ...........................................
- ☐ ...........................................
- ☐ ...........................................
- ☐ ...........................................

# Travel Journal

bon ♡
Voyage

## Places to Mingle :

- ☐ .............................
- ☐ .............................
- ☐ .............................
- ☐ .............................
- ☐ .............................
- ☐ .............................

## Shops to Visit :

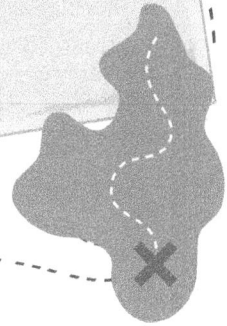

- ☐ .............................
- ☐ .............................
- ☐ .............................
- ☐ .............................
- ☐ .............................
- ☐ .............................
- ☐ .............................

place your
photo here

place your
photo here

# Travel Journal

bon ♡ Voyage

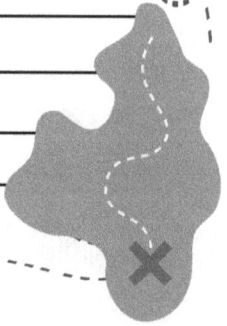

# Travel Journal

## Things to See & Do.

- ☐ .......................................................
- ☐ .......................................................
- ☐ .......................................................
- ☐ .......................................................
- ☐ .......................................................
- ☐ .......................................................
- ☐ .......................................................
- ☐ .......................................................
- ☐ .......................................................
- ☐ .......................................................

## Adventures to Have :

- ☐ .......................................................
- ☐ .......................................................
- ☐ .......................................................
- ☐ .......................................................
- ☐ .......................................................
- ☐ .......................................................
- ☐ .......................................................

## Things to Observe :

- ☐ .......................................................
- ☐ .......................................................
- ☐ .......................................................
- ☐ .......................................................
- ☐ .......................................................
- ☐ .......................................................
- ☐ .......................................................

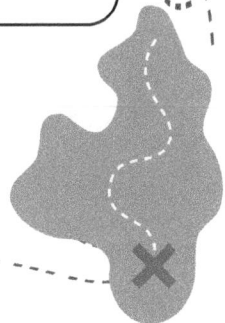

# Travel Journal

## Places to Mingle :

- ☐ ................................................
- ☐ ................................................
- ☐ ................................................
- ☐ ................................................
- ☐ ................................................
- ☐ ................................................

## Shops to Visit :

- ☐ ................................................
- ☐ ................................................
- ☐ ................................................
- ☐ ................................................
- ☐ ................................................
- ☐ ................................................
- ☐ ................................................

place your
photo here

place your
photo here

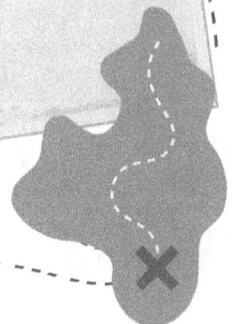

bon ♡
Voyage

# Travel Journal

_____
_____
_____
_____
_____
_____
_____
_____
_____
_____
_____
_____
_____
_____
_____
_____

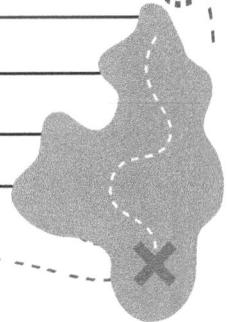

# Travel Journal

## Things to See & Do:

- ☐ ................................................................
- ☐ ................................................................
- ☐ ................................................................
- ☐ ................................................................
- ☐ ................................................................
- ☐ ................................................................
- ☐ ................................................................
- ☐ ................................................................
- ☐ ................................................................

## Adventures to Have :

- ☐ ....................................................
- ☐ ....................................................
- ☐ ....................................................
- ☐ ....................................................
- ☐ ....................................................
- ☐ ....................................................
- ☐ ....................................................

## Things to Observe :

- ☐ ....................................................
- ☐ ....................................................
- ☐ ....................................................
- ☐ ....................................................
- ☐ ....................................................
- ☐ ....................................................
- ☐ ....................................................

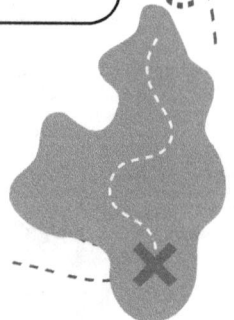

bon Voyage

# Travel Journal

bon ♡ Voyage

## Places to Mingle :

- ☐ ......................................................
- ☐ ......................................................
- ☐ ......................................................
- ☐ ......................................................
- ☐ ......................................................
- ☐ ......................................................
- ☐ ......................................................

## Shops to Visit :

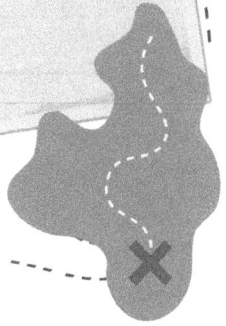

- ☐ ......................................................
- ☐ ......................................................
- ☐ ......................................................
- ☐ ......................................................
- ☐ ......................................................
- ☐ ......................................................
- ☐ ......................................................

place your
photo here

place your
photo here

# Travel Journal

bon Voyage

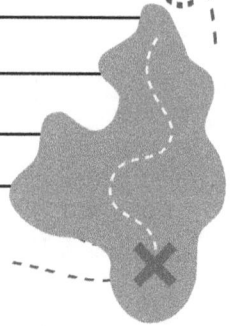

# Travel Journal

## Things to See & Do:

- ☐ .................................................................
- ☐ .................................................................
- ☐ .................................................................
- ☐ .................................................................
- ☐ .................................................................
- ☐ .................................................................
- ☐ .................................................................
- ☐ .................................................................
- ☐ .................................................................
- ☐ .................................................................

## Adventures to Have :

- ☐ ...........................................
- ☐ ...........................................
- ☐ ...........................................
- ☐ ...........................................
- ☐ ...........................................
- ☐ ...........................................

## Things to Observe :

- ☐ ...........................................
- ☐ ...........................................
- ☐ ...........................................
- ☐ ...........................................
- ☐ ...........................................
- ☐ ...........................................
- ☐ ...........................................

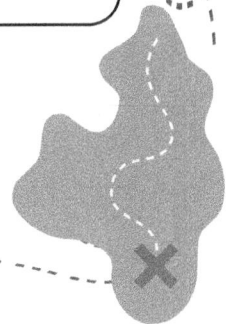

# Travel Journal

bon ♡ Voyage

## Places to Mingle :

☐ ......................................
☐ ......................................
☐ ......................................
☐ ......................................
☐ ......................................
☐ ......................................
☐ ......................................

## Shops to Visit :

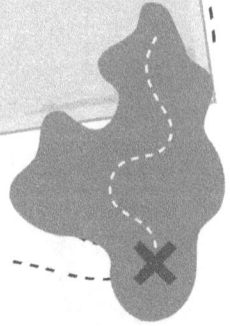

☐ ......................................
☐ ......................................
☐ ......................................
☐ ......................................
☐ ......................................
☐ ......................................
☐ ......................................

place your
photo here

place your
photo here

# Travel Journal

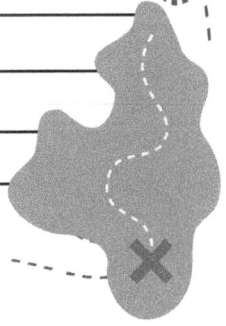

# Travel Journal

bon Voyage

## Things to See & Do:

- ☐ ..................................................................
- ☐ ..................................................................
- ☐ ..................................................................
- ☐ ..................................................................
- ☐ ..................................................................
- ☐ ..................................................................
- ☐ ..................................................................
- ☐ ..................................................................
- ☐ ..................................................................
- ☐ ..................................................................

## Things to Observe:

- ☐ ..................................................................
- ☐ ..................................................................
- ☐ ..................................................................
- ☐ ..................................................................
- ☐ ..................................................................
- ☐ ..................................................................
- ☐ ..................................................................

## Adventures to Have:

- ☐ ..................................................................
- ☐ ..................................................................
- ☐ ..................................................................
- ☐ ..................................................................
- ☐ ..................................................................
- ☐ ..................................................................
- ☐ ..................................................................

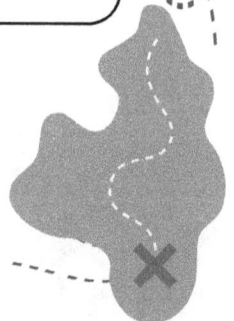

# Travel Journal

bon Voyage

## Places to Mingle :

☐ ..............................................
☐ ..............................................
☐ ..............................................
☐ ..............................................
☐ ..............................................
☐ ..............................................
☐ ..............................................

## Shops to Visit :

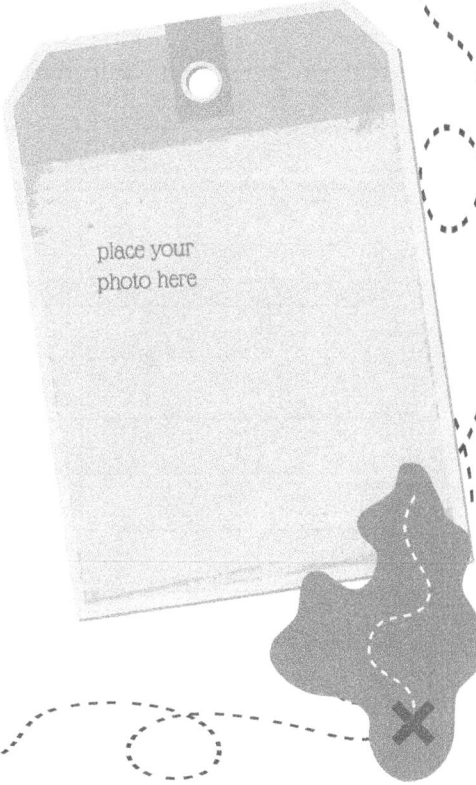

☐ ..............................................
☐ ..............................................
☐ ..............................................
☐ ..............................................
☐ ..............................................
☐ ..............................................
☐ ..............................................

place your
photo here

place your
photo here

# Travel Journal

bon ♡ Voyage

_____

_____

_____

_____

_____

_____

_____

_____

_____

_____

_____

_____

_____

_____

_____

_____

_____

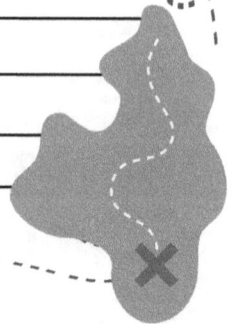

# Travel Journal

bon ♡ Voyage

### Things to See & Do:

- ☐ ......................................................................
- ☐ ......................................................................
- ☐ ......................................................................
- ☐ ......................................................................
- ☐ ......................................................................
- ☐ ......................................................................
- ☐ ......................................................................
- ☐ ......................................................................
- ☐ ......................................................................
- ☐ ......................................................................

### Things to Observe :

- ☐ ........................................
- ☐ ........................................
- ☐ ........................................
- ☐ ........................................
- ☐ ........................................
- ☐ ........................................
- ☐ ........................................

### Adventures to Have :

- ☐ ........................................
- ☐ ........................................
- ☐ ........................................
- ☐ ........................................
- ☐ ........................................
- ☐ ........................................
- ☐ ........................................

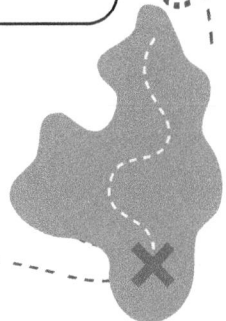

# Travel Journal

bon ♡ Voyage

## Places to Mingle :

- [ ] ....................................
- [ ] ....................................
- [ ] ....................................
- [ ] ....................................
- [ ] ....................................
- [ ] ....................................
- [ ] ....................................

## Shops to Visit :

- [ ] ....................................
- [ ] ....................................
- [ ] ....................................
- [ ] ....................................
- [ ] ....................................
- [ ] ....................................
- [ ] ....................................

place your
photo here

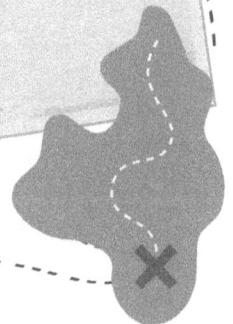

place your
photo here

# Travel Journal

bon Voyage

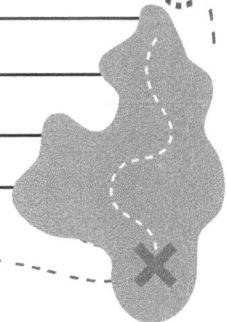

# Travel Journal

## Things to See & Do.

- ☐ .................................................................................
- ☐ .................................................................................
- ☐ .................................................................................
- ☐ .................................................................................
- ☐ .................................................................................
- ☐ .................................................................................
- ☐ .................................................................................
- ☐ .................................................................................
- ☐ .................................................................................
- ☐ .................................................................................

## Adventures to Have :

- ☐ .....................................................
- ☐ .....................................................
- ☐ .....................................................
- ☐ .....................................................
- ☐ .....................................................
- ☐ .....................................................
- ☐ .....................................................

## Things to Observe :

- ☐ .....................................................
- ☐ .....................................................
- ☐ .....................................................
- ☐ .....................................................
- ☐ .....................................................
- ☐ .....................................................
- ☐ .....................................................

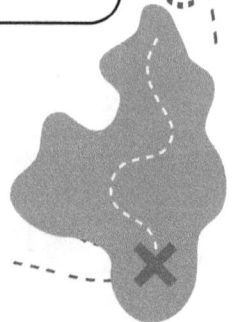

# Travel Journal

## Places to Mingle :

- ☐ .....................................................
- ☐ .....................................................
- ☐ .....................................................
- ☐ .....................................................
- ☐ .....................................................
- ☐ .....................................................
- ☐ .....................................................

## Shops to Visit :

- ☐ .....................................................
- ☐ .....................................................
- ☐ .....................................................
- ☐ .....................................................
- ☐ .....................................................
- ☐ .....................................................
- ☐ .....................................................

place your
photo here

place your
photo here

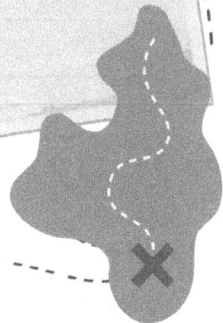

# Travel Journal

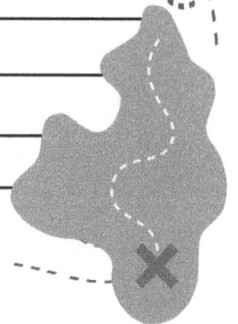

# Travel Journal

## Things to See & Do:

- ☐ ........................................................................
- ☐ ........................................................................
- ☐ ........................................................................
- ☐ ........................................................................
- ☐ ........................................................................
- ☐ ........................................................................
- ☐ ........................................................................
- ☐ ........................................................................
- ☐ ........................................................................
- ☐ ........................................................................

## Things to Observe :

- ☐ ........................................................
- ☐ ........................................................
- ☐ ........................................................
- ☐ ........................................................
- ☐ ........................................................
- ☐ ........................................................
- ☐ ........................................................

## Adventures to Have :

- ☐ ........................................................
- ☐ ........................................................
- ☐ ........................................................
- ☐ ........................................................
- ☐ ........................................................
- ☐ ........................................................
- ☐ ........................................................

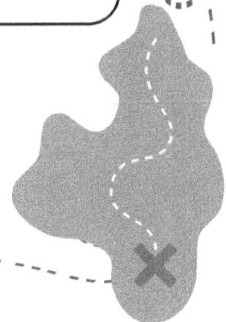

# Travel Journal

bon ♡ Voyage

## Places to Mingle :

- [ ] ......................................
- [ ] ......................................
- [ ] ......................................
- [ ] ......................................
- [ ] ......................................
- [ ] ......................................
- [ ] ......................................

## Shops to Visit :

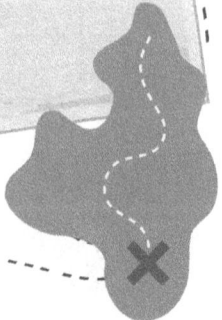

- [ ] ......................................
- [ ] ......................................
- [ ] ......................................
- [ ] ......................................
- [ ] ......................................
- [ ] ......................................
- [ ] ......................................

place your
photo here

place your
photo here

# Travel Journal

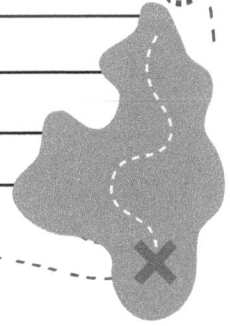

# Travel Journal

bon ♡ Voyage

## Things to See & Do:

- ☐ ............................................................
- ☐ ............................................................
- ☐ ............................................................
- ☐ ............................................................
- ☐ ............................................................
- ☐ ............................................................
- ☐ ............................................................
- ☐ ............................................................
- ☐ ............................................................
- ☐ ............................................................

## Adventures to Have :

- ☐ ...................................
- ☐ ...................................
- ☐ ...................................
- ☐ ...................................
- ☐ ...................................
- ☐ ...................................
- ☐ ...................................

## Things to Observe :

- ☐ ...................................
- ☐ ...................................
- ☐ ...................................
- ☐ ...................................
- ☐ ...................................
- ☐ ...................................
- ☐ ...................................

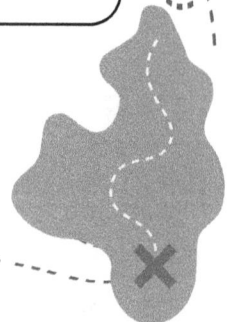

# Travel Journal

**bon♡ Voyage**

## Places to Mingle :

☐ ...................................
☐ ...................................
☐ ...................................
☐ ...................................
☐ ...................................
☐ ...................................

## Shops to Visit :

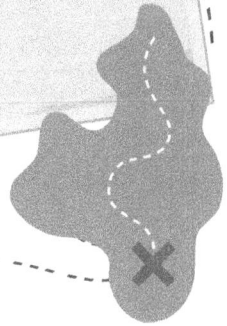

☐ ...................................
☐ ...................................
☐ ...................................
☐ ...................................
☐ ...................................
☐ ...................................
☐ ...................................

place your
photo here

place your
photo here

# Travel Journal

bon♡
Voyage

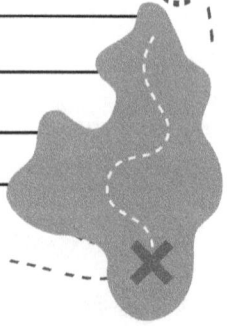

# Travel Journal

bon♡ Voyage

## Things to See & Do:

☐ ..........................................................................
☐ ..........................................................................
☐ ..........................................................................
☐ ..........................................................................
☐ ..........................................................................
☐ ..........................................................................
☐ ..........................................................................
☐ ..........................................................................
☐ ..........................................................................
☐ ..........................................................................

## Things to Observe :

☐ ..........................................................
☐ ..........................................................
☐ ..........................................................
☐ ..........................................................
☐ ..........................................................
☐ ..........................................................
☐ ..........................................................

## Adventures to Have :

☐ ..........................................................
☐ ..........................................................
☐ ..........................................................
☐ ..........................................................
☐ ..........................................................
☐ ..........................................................
☐ ..........................................................

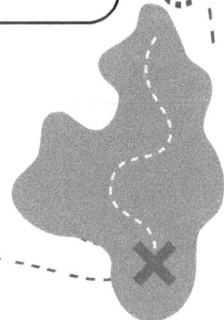

# Travel Journal

## Places to Mingle :

- ☐ ...............................................
- ☐ ...............................................
- ☐ ...............................................
- ☐ ...............................................
- ☐ ...............................................
- ☐ ...............................................
- ☐ ...............................................

## Shops to Visit :

- ☐ ...............................................
- ☐ ...............................................
- ☐ ...............................................
- ☐ ...............................................
- ☐ ...............................................
- ☐ ...............................................
- ☐ ...............................................

place your
photo here

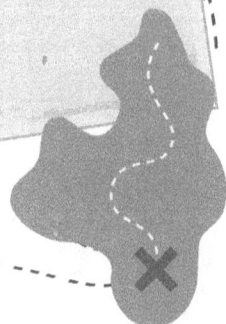

place your
photo here

# Travel Journal

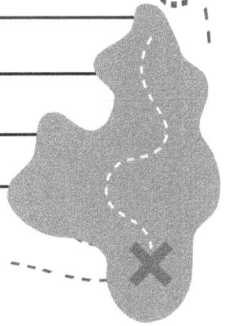

# Travel Journal

## Things to See & Do:

- ☐ ............................................................
- ☐ ............................................................
- ☐ ............................................................
- ☐ ............................................................
- ☐ ............................................................
- ☐ ............................................................
- ☐ ............................................................
- ☐ ............................................................
- ☐ ............................................................

## Adventures to Have :

- ☐ ...................................
- ☐ ...................................
- ☐ ...................................
- ☐ ...................................
- ☐ ...................................
- ☐ ...................................
- ☐ ...................................

## Things to Observe :

- ☐ ...................................
- ☐ ...................................
- ☐ ...................................
- ☐ ...................................
- ☐ ...................................
- ☐ ...................................

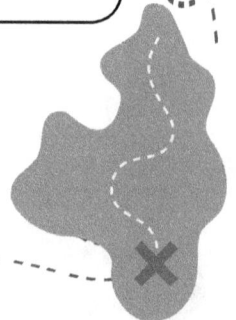

# Travel Journal

bon ♡
Voyage

## Shops to Visit :

☐ ....................................................
☐ ....................................................
☐ ....................................................
☐ ....................................................
☐ ....................................................
☐ ....................................................
☐ ....................................................

## Places to Mingle :

☐ ....................................................
☐ ....................................................
☐ ....................................................
☐ ....................................................
☐ ....................................................
☐ ....................................................
☐ ....................................................

place your
photo here

place your
photo here

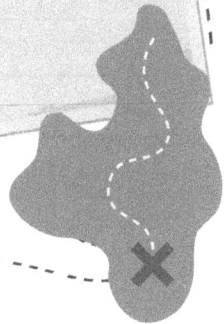

# Travel Journal

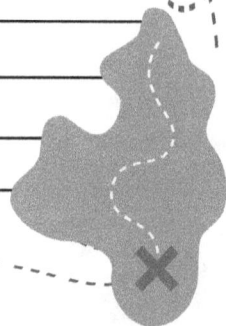

# Travel Journal

## Things to See & Do:

- ☐ ....................................................................
- ☐ ....................................................................
- ☐ ....................................................................
- ☐ ....................................................................
- ☐ ....................................................................
- ☐ ....................................................................
- ☐ ....................................................................
- ☐ ....................................................................
- ☐ ....................................................................
- ☐ ....................................................................

## Adventures to Have :

- ☐ ..............................................
- ☐ ..............................................
- ☐ ..............................................
- ☐ ..............................................
- ☐ ..............................................
- ☐ ..............................................
- ☐ ..............................................

## Things to Observe :

- ☐ ..............................................
- ☐ ..............................................
- ☐ ..............................................
- ☐ ..............................................
- ☐ ..............................................
- ☐ ..............................................
- ☐ ..............................................

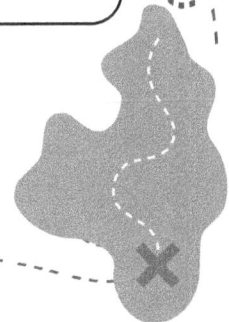

# Travel Journal

bon ♡ Voyage

## Places to Mingle :

- ☐ .............................................
- ☐ .............................................
- ☐ .............................................
- ☐ .............................................
- ☐ .............................................
- ☐ .............................................

## Shops to Visit :

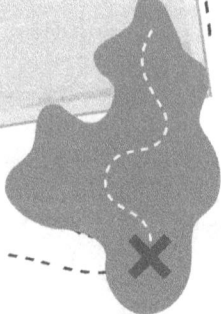

- ☐ .............................................
- ☐ .............................................
- ☐ .............................................
- ☐ .............................................
- ☐ .............................................
- ☐ .............................................
- ☐ .............................................

place your
photo here

place your
photo here

# Travel Journal

bon Voyage

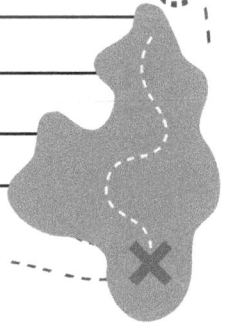

# Travel Journal

bon Voyage

## Things to See & Do:

- [ ] ......................................................................
- [ ] ......................................................................
- [ ] ......................................................................
- [ ] ......................................................................
- [ ] ......................................................................
- [ ] ......................................................................
- [ ] ......................................................................
- [ ] ......................................................................
- [ ] ......................................................................
- [ ] ......................................................................

## Adventures to Have :

- [ ] ...................................
- [ ] ...................................
- [ ] ...................................
- [ ] ...................................
- [ ] ...................................
- [ ] ...................................
- [ ] ...................................

## Things to Observe :

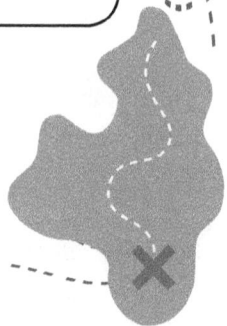

- [ ] ...................................
- [ ] ...................................
- [ ] ...................................
- [ ] ...................................
- [ ] ...................................
- [ ] ...................................

# Travel Journal

bon ♡ Voyage

## Places to Mingle :

☐ ...........................................
☐ ...........................................
☐ ...........................................
☐ ...........................................
☐ ...........................................
☐ ...........................................
☐ ...........................................

## Shops to Visit :

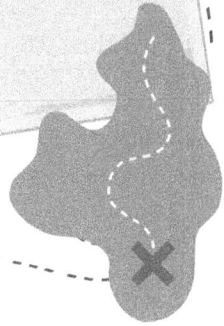

☐ ...........................................
☐ ...........................................
☐ ...........................................
☐ ...........................................
☐ ...........................................
☐ ...........................................
☐ ...........................................

place your
photo here

place your
photo here

# Travel Journal

_____

_____

_____

_____

_____

_____

_____

_____

_____

_____

_____

_____

_____

_____

_____

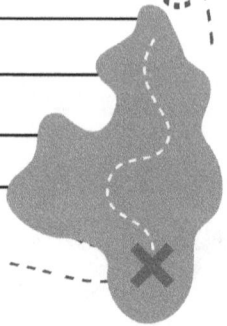

# Travel Journal

bon ♡ Voyage

## Things to See & Do:

- ☐ .............................................................
- ☐ .............................................................
- ☐ .............................................................
- ☐ .............................................................
- ☐ .............................................................
- ☐ .............................................................
- ☐ .............................................................
- ☐ .............................................................
- ☐ .............................................................
- ☐ .............................................................

## Things to Observe :

- ☐ ....................................
- ☐ ....................................
- ☐ ....................................
- ☐ ....................................
- ☐ ....................................
- ☐ ....................................
- ☐ ....................................

## Adventures to Have :

- ☐ ....................................
- ☐ ....................................
- ☐ ....................................
- ☐ ....................................
- ☐ ....................................
- ☐ ....................................
- ☐ ....................................

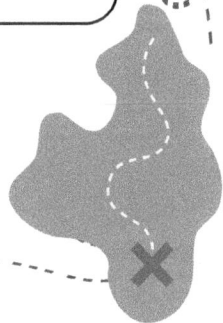

# Travel Journal

bon♡
Voyage

### Places to Mingle :

☐ .................................................
☐ .................................................
☐ .................................................
☐ .................................................
☐ .................................................
☐ .................................................

### Shops to Visit :

☐ .................................................
☐ .................................................
☐ .................................................
☐ .................................................
☐ .................................................
☐ .................................................
☐ .................................................

place your
photo here

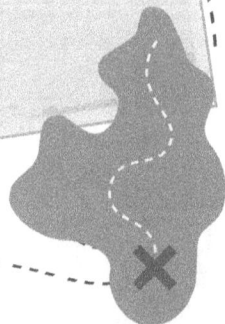

place your
photo here

# Travel Journal

bon ♡ Voyage

# Travel Journal

bon Voyage

## Things to See & Do:

- ☐ ......................................................
- ☐ ......................................................
- ☐ ......................................................
- ☐ ......................................................
- ☐ ......................................................
- ☐ ......................................................
- ☐ ......................................................
- ☐ ......................................................
- ☐ ......................................................
- ☐ ......................................................

## Adventures to Have :

- ☐ ......................................
- ☐ ......................................
- ☐ ......................................
- ☐ ......................................
- ☐ ......................................
- ☐ ......................................
- ☐ ......................................

## Things to Observe :

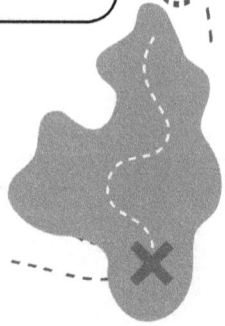

- ☐ ......................................
- ☐ ......................................
- ☐ ......................................
- ☐ ......................................
- ☐ ......................................
- ☐ ......................................
- ☐ ......................................

# Travel Journal

bon♡ Voyage

## Places to Mingle :

☐ .................................
☐ .................................
☐ .................................
☐ .................................
☐ .................................
☐ .................................
☐ .................................

## Shops to Visit :

☐ .................................
☐ .................................
☐ .................................
☐ .................................
☐ .................................
☐ .................................
☐ .................................

place your
photo here

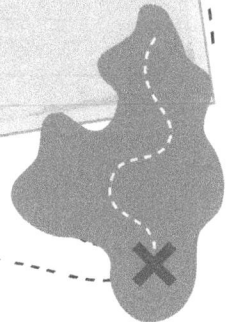

place your
photo here

# Travel Journal

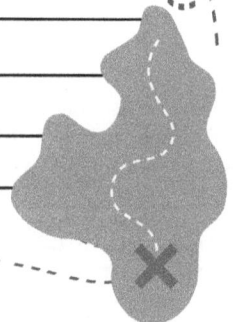

bon ♡ Voyage

# Travel Journal

bon Voyage

## Things to See & Do:

- ☐ ..................................................................
- ☐ ..................................................................
- ☐ ..................................................................
- ☐ ..................................................................
- ☐ ..................................................................
- ☐ ..................................................................
- ☐ ..................................................................
- ☐ ..................................................................
- ☐ ..................................................................
- ☐ ..................................................................

## Things to Observe :

- ☐ ..................................................
- ☐ ..................................................
- ☐ ..................................................
- ☐ ..................................................
- ☐ ..................................................
- ☐ ..................................................
- ☐ ..................................................

## Adventures to Have :

- ☐ ..................................................
- ☐ ..................................................
- ☐ ..................................................
- ☐ ..................................................
- ☐ ..................................................
- ☐ ..................................................

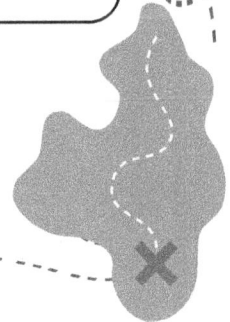

# Travel Journal

bon ♡ Voyage

## Places to Mingle :

☐ ..................................
☐ ..................................
☐ ..................................
☐ ..................................
☐ ..................................
☐ ..................................
☐ ..................................

## Shops to Visit :

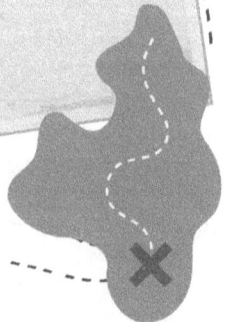

☐ ..................................
☐ ..................................
☐ ..................................
☐ ..................................
☐ ..................................
☐ ..................................
☐ ..................................

place your
photo here

place your
photo here

# Travel Journal

bon Voyage

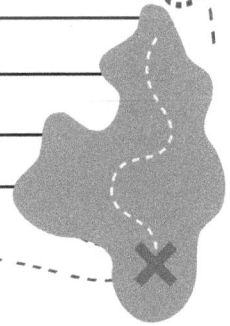

# Travel Journal

bon♡ Voyage

## Things to See & Do:

- ☐ .................................................
- ☐ .................................................
- ☐ .................................................
- ☐ .................................................
- ☐ .................................................
- ☐ .................................................
- ☐ .................................................
- ☐ .................................................
- ☐ .................................................
- ☐ .................................................

## Adventures to Have :

- ☐ ...........................................
- ☐ ...........................................
- ☐ ...........................................
- ☐ ...........................................
- ☐ ...........................................
- ☐ ...........................................
- ☐ ...........................................

## Things to Observe :

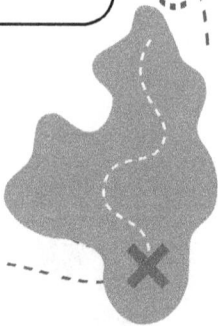

- ☐ ...........................................
- ☐ ...........................................
- ☐ ...........................................
- ☐ ...........................................
- ☐ ...........................................
- ☐ ...........................................
- ☐ ...........................................

# Travel Journal

bon ♡ Voyage

## Places to Mingle :

☐ .........................................
☐ .........................................
☐ .........................................
☐ .........................................
☐ .........................................
☐ .........................................
☐ .........................................

## Shops to Visit :

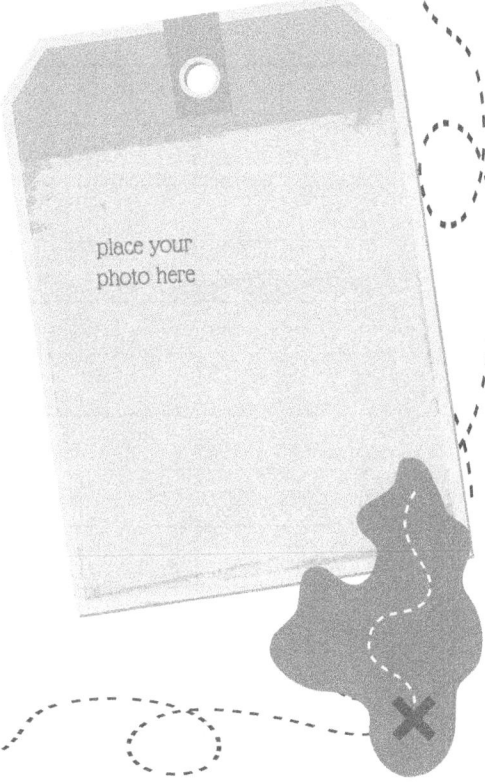

☐ .........................................
☐ .........................................
☐ .........................................
☐ .........................................
☐ .........................................
☐ .........................................
☐ .........................................

place your
photo here

place your
photo here

# Travel Journal

bon ♡
Voyage

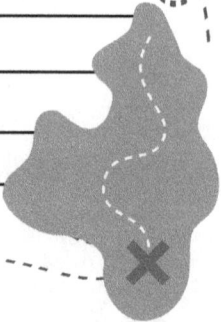

# Travel Journal

## Things to See & Do:

- ☐ ..................................................................
- ☐ ..................................................................
- ☐ ..................................................................
- ☐ ..................................................................
- ☐ ..................................................................
- ☐ ..................................................................
- ☐ ..................................................................
- ☐ ..................................................................
- ☐ ..................................................................
- ☐ ..................................................................

## Adventures to Have :

- ☐ ..................................................
- ☐ ..................................................
- ☐ ..................................................
- ☐ ..................................................
- ☐ ..................................................
- ☐ ..................................................
- ☐ ..................................................

## Things to Observe :

- ☐ ..................................................
- ☐ ..................................................
- ☐ ..................................................
- ☐ ..................................................
- ☐ ..................................................
- ☐ ..................................................
- ☐ ..................................................

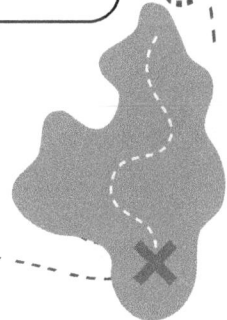

# Travel Journal

bon ♡ Voyage

## Places to Mingle :

- ☐ ......................................
- ☐ ......................................
- ☐ ......................................
- ☐ ......................................
- ☐ ......................................
- ☐ ......................................

## Shops to Visit :

- ☐ ......................................
- ☐ ......................................
- ☐ ......................................
- ☐ ......................................
- ☐ ......................................
- ☐ ......................................
- ☐ ......................................

place your
photo here

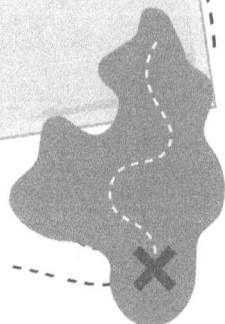

place your
photo here

# Travel Journal

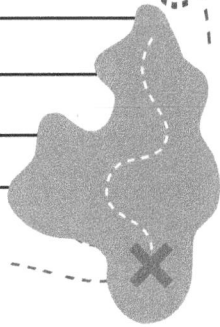

bon ♡ Voyage

# Travel Journal

bon ♡ Voyage

## Things to See & Do:

- ☐ ........................................................
- ☐ ........................................................
- ☐ ........................................................
- ☐ ........................................................
- ☐ ........................................................
- ☐ ........................................................
- ☐ ........................................................
- ☐ ........................................................
- ☐ ........................................................
- ☐ ........................................................

## Things to Observe :

- ☐ ........................................
- ☐ ........................................
- ☐ ........................................
- ☐ ........................................
- ☐ ........................................
- ☐ ........................................
- ☐ ........................................

## Adventures to Have :

- ☐ ........................................
- ☐ ........................................
- ☐ ........................................
- ☐ ........................................
- ☐ ........................................
- ☐ ........................................
- ☐ ........................................

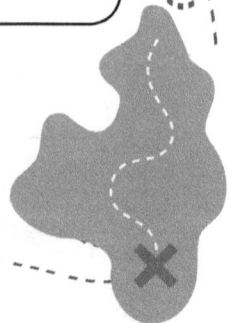

# Travel Journal

bon♡ Voyage

## Places to Mingle :

- ☐ .................................................
- ☐ .................................................
- ☐ .................................................
- ☐ .................................................
- ☐ .................................................
- ☐ .................................................
- ☐ .................................................

## Shops to Visit :

- ☐ .................................................
- ☐ .................................................
- ☐ .................................................
- ☐ .................................................
- ☐ .................................................
- ☐ .................................................
- ☐ .................................................

place your
photo here

place your
photo here

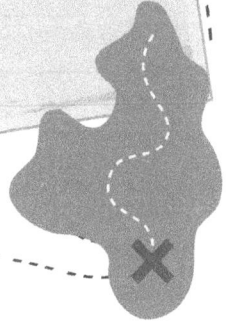

# Travel Journal

bon Voyage

_____
_____
_____
_____
_____
_____
_____
_____
_____
_____
_____
_____
_____
_____
_____

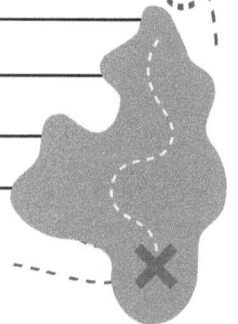

# Travel Journal

## Things to See & Do:

- ☐ ...........................................................
- ☐ ...........................................................
- ☐ ...........................................................
- ☐ ...........................................................
- ☐ ...........................................................
- ☐ ...........................................................
- ☐ ...........................................................
- ☐ ...........................................................
- ☐ ...........................................................
- ☐ ...........................................................

## Adventures to Have :

- ☐ ...........................................
- ☐ ...........................................
- ☐ ...........................................
- ☐ ...........................................
- ☐ ...........................................
- ☐ ...........................................
- ☐ ...........................................

## Things to Observe :

- ☐ ...........................................
- ☐ ...........................................
- ☐ ...........................................
- ☐ ...........................................
- ☐ ...........................................
- ☐ ...........................................
- ☐ ...........................................

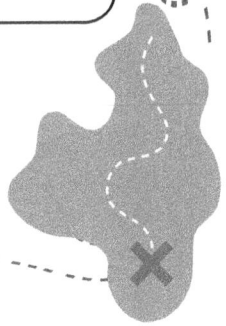

# Travel Journal

bon ♡ Voyage

## Places to Mingle :

☐ .......................................
☐ .......................................
☐ .......................................
☐ .......................................
☐ .......................................
☐ .......................................
☐ .......................................

## Shops to Visit :

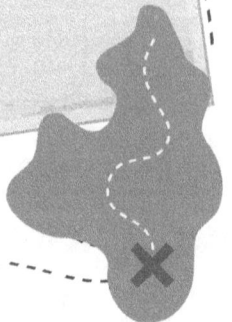

☐ .......................................
☐ .......................................
☐ .......................................
☐ .......................................
☐ .......................................
☐ .......................................
☐ .......................................

place your
photo here

place your
photo here

# Travel Journal

bon Voyage

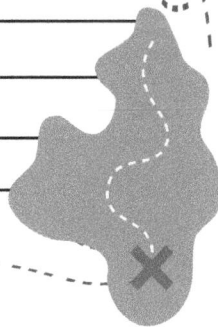

www.ingramcontent.com/pod-product-compliance
Lightning Source LLC
Chambersburg PA
CBHW081333090426
42737CB00017B/3129